GROWING UP CHRISTIAN IN A SEXY WORLD

by Cinda Warner Gorman

DEDICATION:

To Steve, my partner in marriage, parenting and ministry. He conceived of and christened this course in 1981 in a different setting for older youth. He freely shared his ideas for me to reshape for an intergenerational course. This is partnership as we experience it — becoming more than we could become alone.

GROWING UP CHRISTIAN IN A SEXY WORLD

Copyright © by EDUCATIONAL MINISTRIES, INC. All rights reserved. Printed in the United States of America. No portion of this book may be reproduced by any means without prior permission of the copyright owner.

ISBN 0-940754-78-9

EDUCATIONAL MINISTRIES, INC.
Brea, California

TABLE OF CONTENTS

INTRODUCTION..5

SESSION 1 — Everyone Has Something to Say About Sex...9

SESSION 2 — Does Everybody Feel As Different As I Do?.17

SESSION 3 — Good Grief — What's Happening to Me?.....23

SESSION 4 — Childhood Sexual Abuse Prevention...........29

ALTERNATE SESSION 4 — Focus on A.I.D.S....................34

SESSION 5 — "How Did I Get Here?"................................37

SESSION 6 — Being Alike, Being Liked, Being Myself.......43

BIBLIOGRAPHY..49

INTRODUCTION

"Growing Up Christian in a Sexy World" is a parent-child class for 5th-6th graders and one parent or significant adult. All of the activities and content presume that the adults will be a part of the instruction in 3 ways:

1. by their presence-willingness to participate
2. by their "askableness"-responding to their child's questions
3. by sharing their own memories and experiences

Neither the parents or leader are expected to be experts. Filmstrips and additional pamphlets may be acquired for content (a bibliography follows). This means you cannot read this manual the week before the class is scheduled to begin and expect to be ready to teach it. Finding materials to borrow, rent, or purchase may take at least a month. During the weeks prior to the course, you may read **Raising a Child Conservatively in a Sexually Permissive World** by Sol and Judith Gordon (Simon/Schuster, 1983) This book is "for parents who want to be the principal sex educators of their children, who want their children to grow up with healthy attitudes and who are not apologetic about wanting to get across their own values." Copies could also be made available for borrowing or purchase by parents.

FORMAT

This class has been taught as a six-week (evening) format and a two week (Saturday morning) format. Each schedule has its advantages—the lengthier format allows for more parent/child dialogue between each lesson and more extensive "homework." The shorter format means few absences and more intense "building upon" each idea.

RESOURCES

Session 1 — magazines read by preteens, teens and families

Session 2 — "Feelings Grow, Too" Part 1 — 13 minutes Filmstrip/cassette

Session 3 — Concordia Sex Education Series — 14 minutes Filmstrip/cassette

    #3 How You Got to Be You, 4-6th grade
    Alternative for synagogue, "Where Did I Come From?" Video

Session 4 — "No More Secrets for Me" by Oralee Watcher. A book of stories to turn into skits
Speaker and brochures about A.I.D.S. available locally

Session 5 — "When Life Begins," 15 minutes, CRM-McGraw Hill Films

Check with local diocese, or interfaith resource centers, school district media centers, or public library audio visual resources.

PREPARATION

At the beginning of each lesson there is a section titled, "PREPARATION." In addition to preparing the content of the lesson, adapting it to your group size and setting, these are things which you need to "plan ahead" for. Read all six of these with your calendar in hand or an assistant who will share some of these "go-fer" tasks. This will leave more time for focusing on the session itself as the day draws near.

USE IN OTHER SETTINGS

This course could be adapted for use in a synagogue or interfaith setting. Alternate resources would be needed for Session 3 and Old Testament examples/scriptures would be needed in Session 6.

ROOM ARRANGEMENT

The room may be arranged in a double horseshoe with kids on the inside ring and their parents on the outside. Participants should have a clear view of a screen. For the first lesson, three tables are needed for working on collages and a fourth table to hold supplies. Sometimes projectors are needed for films and filmstrips. A blackboard or newsprint pad should be visible. For the fourth lesson, you will need some places for parents to prepare skits. Inexpensive lap boards for doing questionnaires would be helpful. You'll also want a cart or table to spread out the handouts for easy accessibility.

PARTICIPANTS

The class is designed for parents and 5th and 6th grade children. The increasing popularity of "middle schools (6th/7th/8th)" means 5th graders need to be better prepared for the "education" they may receive from increasingly older peers during their next school year. Families with two children in this age group should be encouraged to bring both parents or bring one child each year. The experience of sharing these subjects one-on-one can be very special.

PUBLICITY

Keep your eyes open for comic strips, cartoons, magazine articles, etc. which can be used for posters and handouts. Make sure the explanation of class participants is clear so parents will accompany their child. The location, time and dates should be convenient to families. (i.e. – not Saturdays during Little League or during Monday Night Football) Emphasize the fun of learning together. A book table and poster display can be used on a sign-up table. Some churches have charged a fee and purchased one book per family or several resources.

SESSION ONE

EVERYBODY HAS SOMETHING TO SAY ABOUT SEX

OBJECTIVE: To find out where we get our impression about sexuality, sex roles, physical sex and what "sexy" is.

PREPARATION:
1. Copy handouts (on two colors for ease of handing)
2. Collect materials and solicit magazines for collages.
3. Borrow a popular rock tape or record a variety from a radio station.

SET UP: Chairs should be arranged in a double horseshoe. Nametags should be available with bright felt-tip markers. Four tables should be set-up with butcher paper labeled for each collage and one table for supplies.

CLASSTIME

A. Ask the children to introduce themselves by saying their name and grade (and school if they come from several sites). Ask the parents to introduce themselves and say the name and location (city) of the elementary school they attended when they were their child's grade.

B. On the board list all the sources (places, media, people) from which class members have received an impression or lesson about sex or sexuality. (i.e. church, big sister, locker room, 4-H, etc.) Briefly define the difference between the terms "sexuality" and "sex". (This is aimed at parents.) It may be printed on newsprint and explained in your own words.

> *"Sexuality is what we're about in terms of love and intimate relationships, masculinity and femininity, feelings and values and attitudes. Sex, according to our usage, refers specifically to a range of sexual activities involving the genitals."* (Gordon/Gordon)

C. Give brief instruction for the next TWO parts.

   1. Parents and kids will each get a separate handout. Fill it out and discuss it in family groups. Chairs may be moved to a twosome or threesome position. Pencils are available on the supply table.

   2. "When you have finished discussing the questionnaires, you may choose one of the three collages to work on. Use the magazines, scissors, glue, etc., to portray what our culture thinks a real man or real woman or really sexy is. Groups may share pictures back and forth between collages to be helpful to one another."

D. Send them off to begin handouts. In about 20 minutes they should be finishing. On a central table, the following materials should be available:

   1. pencils (for questionnaire)
   2. scissors
   3. glue, paste, rubber cement or glue sticks
   4. current magazines (both teen & adult—solicit contributions from participants, your senior high and junior high groups and neighbors)
   5. masking tape

Title three large butcher paper sheets and put on tables. When just about everyone is working on a collage, you may want to play a tape or record of popular music.

E. In about 15 minutes, a group of 20 can create 3 collages worth hanging up. Display them and ask for their impressions—did they find anything they disagreed with? What did the women usually sell? What did men sell? Had parents ever seen teen magazines? How were men and women used differently?

F. If you haven't already done so, return to the horseshoe with handouts. Take a quick break for parents to give kids a neck rub, then share some of the lighter answers from the questionnaires—look for trends.

G. Read from the Creation account and focus on Genesis 1:27, 28ff, stressing that our sexuality was given by God and is very good.

H. Preview the upcoming lessons. Prepare parents to find baby pictures to bring to Session 4. Pictures of both parents and their child should be submitted. Suggest they write down a description of two commercials from TV or two MTV segments that used sex in a way that doesn't correspond with God's judgment of sex as "very good."

I. Make the horseshoe into a circle for a closing prayer. Return nametags to a central place and be dismissed.

Be sure to save the collages for Session 6.

Session I Handout

FOR KIDS

Fill out the following as quickly as you can...you will share your answers with others if that makes a difference in what you say.

Five things I talk about with my friends are:

Five things I talk about with my dad are:

Five things I talk about with my mom are:

If I could get an honest answer, I would ask my best friend:

If I could get an honest answer, I would ask my parents:

If I could wave a magic wand and be older, I would like to be _____ because:

If I could wave a magic wand and be younger, I would like to be _____ because:

The best thing about my age now is:

The worst things about my age now is:

The most fun time I ever remember having with my family was when:

If I could pick one day in my life to live over again, it would be:

Session I Handout

FOR PARENTS

Fill out the following as quickly as you can...you will share your answers with others if that makes a difference in what you say.

Five things I talk about with my friends:

Five things I talk about with my kids:

If I could get an honest answer, I would ask a friend:

If I could get an honest answer, I would ask my child (here today):

If I could wave a magic wand and be younger, I would like to be _____ because:

If I could wave a magic wand and be older, I would like to be _____ because:

The best thing about my age now is:

The worst thing about my age now is:

The most fun time I ever remember having with my family while I was growing up was:

If I could pick one day in my life to live over again, it would be:

Supplement to session one — for information/viewpoint

DOES SEX SELL ADVERTISING?

"We live in a culture in which men derive their identity from proving that they are strong...so in advertising, as in other areas, men tend to play to that cultural reality that has been so ingrained in them. And it's reflected in the advertising that we see."
— Patricia Carbine, publisher and editor-in-chief, Ms. Magazine

The Lancome skin creme advertising shows a beautiful woman in bed, seemingly in the throes of sexual ecstasy.

A Calvin Klein ad pictures a couple in the grips of torrid, passionate lovemaking.

A woman in a Canadian Club whiskey ad looks calculatingly seductive. "Be a part of it," reads the ad's catch line.

The subject is sex in advertising and, while two observers of the advertising industry differ on the extent to which explicit sexual images of women are used to sell everything from tires to toilet tissue, they both agree that the problem is slowly improving. Advertising agencies are beginning to realize that "women don't respond to advertisements that go from the romantic, sexy and erotic over the line into what is really pornographic," said Patricia Carbine, publisher and editor-in-chief of Ms. Magazine.

"I've always believed that advertising that people like and respond to positively is going to sell better than advertising that offends or insults their intelligence — including advertising that exploits the bodies men and women," added John O'Toole, chairman of Foote, Cone and Belding Communications Inc., whose clients include Levi, Clorox, Arco and Mazda.

Carbine and O'Toole were among numerous advertising executives attending the American Association of Advertising Agencies' Western Region Convention last weekend at the Hotel del Coronado. While criticizing some print advertisements — most from the fashion industry — that use female images "to embrace sexual violence and pseudo-violence," Carbine singled out Calvin Klein jean ads as the "most deeply disturbing and distressing."

"The models in these ads are usually extremely young girls. The implicit message is that if you can't exploit older women, the next thing is to turn into sex objects are teens," she said. "It's irresponsible." Advertisements in women's fashion magazines also frequently go beyond the bounds of propriety, Carbine said. "I turn the pages of Vogue and see ads in which a gun is in the corner, a woman's arm is in the clasp of a Doberman's jaws. They're highly stylized, often stunning photographic images that picture women victimized, or about to be victimized," she said. Carbine stressed that it isn't always restricted to the exploitation of female images.

"There is a very large men's underwear poster that I see in the bus shelters in New York that is fairly explicit. More than a few men I've talked with are uncomfortable about having to stand near those posters," she said. And male bodies "objectified" for the sake of titillation, she believes, have the same effect on consumers as do erotic advertisements featuring women. "These irritating, condescending and insulting ads aren't going to help in selling products," she said, adding that Ms. Magazine occasionally turns down clients' advertising that it finds objectionable. "The products that do sell will make it in spite of the advertising."

Much of the problem, Carbine believes, is the same as in most American institutions: The majority of decisions still are made by men. "We live in a culture in which men derive their identity from proving that they are strong and that they are capable of taking violent actions in order to prove their manhood," she said. "So in advertising, as in other areas, men tend to play to that cultural reality that has been so ingrained in them. And it's reflected in the advertising that we see."

The remedy, she said, may lie in the self-policing of ads by the advertising industry. "Young people, especially, get much of their social cues and cultural cues from advertising," she said. "To say that they don't act upon these cues is to deny reality. As media figures, we need to take some sort of responsibility for the problem."

John O'Toole, author of the book, **The Trouble With Advertising,** *said that he looks at explicit advertising like a glass half-full of water. "We are moving toward portraying women in their more realistic roles of family and society," he said. "We're not perfect yet, but we've come giant steps in the last few years."*

Like Carbine, O'Toole criticized the Calvin Klein jean ads as "sexual exploitation." "But I think that the ads were aimed at getting the attention of clothing distributors, rather than selling to consumers," he said. "Being involved as I am in creating the advertising for Levi's, I can say that it was certainly no way to sell jeans." Even in men's magazines — such as Penthouse, Playboy and Esquire — ads that use women as "sex bait" to sell products, O'Toole said, are probably not effective. "I think that most men today, after realizing that such ads also exploit them, feel cheated enough to move on to the next page," he said.

O'Toole, 55, acknowledged that rock music videos — many of which have been criticized for sexually exploiting images of women — are having a profound effect on the advertising industry. "The fast pace, the colors, the unusual situation are the sort of things we picked up on for our Levi's 501 ads," he said. "But many of the rock videos also have a negative side to them. There are some very disturbing things going on that I doubt will be translated into ads directed at the general audience." Some rock videos shown on MTV (the Music Television network) have depicted women in threatening situations. One video shows a woman running down a dark street with a worried look on her face, followed close behind by a rock band singing an implicitly sexual song.

"More and more, even the most recalcitrant advertisers realize that you don't make a profit by associating your product with messages that offend or insult people," he said.

Used by permission: The San Diego Union by Frank Green, staff writer.

SESSION TWO

DOES EVERYBODY FEEL AS DIFFERENT AS I DO?

OBJECTIVE: To discuss emotional changes, how they are part of God's plan for our lives and what these emotions are getting us ready for.

PREPARATION:
1. copy handouts on different colors
2. rent filmstrip

SETUP: Nametags should be laid out on a table in alphabetical order for people to pick up on their way in. The room can be arranged in any way that all can see a front screen. Pencils and lap boards should be available unless people move to tables for handout work. As people drift in, you may begin hearing what they saw on television during the week. See if they were more sensitized to the issue of sex in advertising because of Session I.

CLASSTIME

A. Begin the session with a stand up, sit-down exercise intended to help all participants see their uniqueness. Simply ask people to stand whenever a word or phrase describes them and sit when it doesn't.

STAND UP...

if you have brown hair...red...blond...gray...purple...none or thinning
if you wear glasses...contact lenses
if you wear braces...used to wear braces
if you like to sing...work in the garden...watch T.V.
prefer big parties...small parties...no parties
like to play ping pong...basketball...(boogie board, ski, etc.)
are under 5 feet tall...over 6 feet...between 5 & 6 feet tall
ever wished your body looked different than it does (shorter, taller, thinner, more muscular)

ASK THE CLASS

"Was there ever a time in that exercise that we all stood up together? Was there one other person who stood up and sat down on exactly the same questions you did?"

B. Expand on the following:

"We are different. We enjoy different things and grow at different rates. Even two children in the same family may grow at different rates and end up at different heights (use your family of origin as an example or another family known to the class).

People also grow emotionally. You used to be afraid of things like loud sirens or big dogs, etc.—you are probably different now. Your feelings change."

Read Luke 2:51 & 52. Remind people that we don't know much about Jesus' growing years. Because so little is said, we can presume there was little that was extraordinary—that he grew and changed like all young boys who become teenagers.

(Substitute I Samuel, Chapter 1 in a synagogue or inter faith setting.)

How many boys/men hated girls in the primary grades?
How many girls/women hated boys in the primary grades?
Do you still feel the same way?

C. Introduce the filmstrip "Feelings Grow, Too" or an equivalent message about emotional changes. After it, ask for their observations/questions.

Session 2 Handout

KID SHEET

Draw a picture of yourself at the age you are today.

Draw a picture of yourself at age 18.

I am _____ years old.

I will be 18 in the year_____.

List three things about yourself now that you feel really good about:

1.
2.
3.

Think about when you will be 18 years old. What will you be like? List three things you think will be good about you when you are 18.

1.
2.
3.

Used by permission. **Growing Up Boys** by Wernette, Hansen and Taylor. Planned Parenthood of Southern Arizona.

Session 2 Handout

PARENT SHEET

Draw a picture of yourself at the age you are today.

Draw a picture of yourself as a 5th or 6th grader.

I am _____ years old.

The year was _____.

List three things about you that make you feel good about yourself.

1.
2.
3.

List three things that were good about you at the earlier age you drew above.

1.
2.
3.

Used by permission. **Growing Up Boys** by Wernette, Hansen and Taylor. Planned Parenthood of Southern Arizona.

D. Do the handouts in family groups. If time allows, share with 2 or 3 family groups together — otherwise limit it to parents with their children.

E. In the closing moments, remind people that they can begin to bring baby pictures next week. Their name should be on the back of the photo and it should be brought in an envelope.

F. Close in a prayer praising God for the special plan God has for each person.

Remind people to return nametags.

You may want to provide a "homework" assignment for parents this week as one way of preparing them for the more frank discussion in the coming weeks. Session 2 "homework handout" is just one possibility. You may prefer your own assignment or provide a book table of selections for parental reading.

Session 2 — Homework for Parents

It will be helpful for you to reflect with your marriage partner (or close friend if you are single) about some of the messages you got about sexuality as a youngster. Certainly the way we heard the topic of sex presented or ignored in home, school, or church as a child affects our attitudes as adults.

Share some of your memories of your early education about sexuality. Did your parents show physical affection for each other in your presence? Were there topics "assigned" to one parent or the other for discussion? Could you or would you ask questions? Was there a godly dimension to conversations about sex? Was sex seen as wholesome or dirty? Were there "skeletons" in the family closet which affected attitudes?

After sharing your memories it would be helpful to see how they have affected your present attitudes toward sexuality and your "comfort level" in talking about it with your child. If you are very uncomfortable your child will sense that. A trip to the public library, a church library, or Planned Parenthood office will provide some resources to help. Sol and Judith Gordon's **Raising Children Conservatively in a Sexually Permissive World** is very helpful. Clifford and Joyce Penner's **The Gift of Sex** is a frank "Christian Guide to Sexual Fulfillment." The third and fourth chapters suggest a wholesome Biblical Perspective. By better understanding and getting comfortable with your own sexuality you will be able to put your child at ease as he or she learns about changing bodies, emotions, and attitudes.

Cliff and Joyce Penner suggest we look to Old Testament characters like Abraham, Jacob and David for examples of heroes of the faith who were people of passion. God accepts us as whole beings who have very strong sexual feelings. We are each an integrated whole and may or may not have been given permission in our growing up years to feel good about the pleasures that come from the good gift of sex.

SESSION THREE

GOOD GRIEF — WHAT'S HAPPENING TO ME?

OBJECTIVE: To get accurate information about physical changes and to hear what the parents remember about their own experiences of puberty.

PREPARATION:
1. copy handouts (kids on both sides)
2. borrow filmstrip — Concordia Sex Education Series #3 "How You Got to Be You" or video "Where Did I Come From?" (synagogue)

SETUP: Establish a central collecting box for baby pictures. Nametags may or may not be necessary by now.

CLASSTIME

A. Begin the session with people in family pairs/threes. Have them begin as follows:

"Now we are going to do some imagining and remembering...recalling changes happening in our children over the past few years. All of us are going to be thinking about kids — kids think about yourselves and parents think about the child who is here with you today. Sit in family groups or pairs."

CLOSE YOUR EYES

"Try to remember what this child looked like at two years old. (Kids you can remember a baby picture you have seen.) Think about the color of their hair, their cheeks (chubby or thin) their arms and how far they came down on the side of their body; think about how big their head was in proportion to their body. Remember a specific outfit they wore at that age." (Proceed slowly — allow time for memory to work.)

"Now let us go back and remember them in Kindergarten at age five or six." (Go through the same steps.)

"Now recall their eighth birthday party — their smile is now full of adult teeth, their hair may have changed color or style."

"You may open your eyes and look at your child. Now see them with a new appreciation for how God plans for their growth...their feet are growing, their head fits their shoulders, their teeth may be ready for the orthodontist and big bills! Their face has probably changed shape somewhat and their arms can now reach all the way over their head and touch their ear on the other side (I don't know what that is good for)."

"Kids, give your folks a hug if you want to. They are the ones who have kept you fed and clothed and loved through all these years to bring you to this point!"

B. Read Ecclesiastes 3:1-11 (TEV). Emphasize the first verse, "Everything that happens in this world happens at the time God chooses," and the eleventh, "He has set the right time for everything. He has given us a desire to know the future, but never gives us the satisfaction of fully understanding what He does." Apply this to our changing bodies and the time clocks inside our God-created bodies which cannot be pushed ahead — boys who think they are too short or girls who want a full figure just have to wait for the time.

C. Pass out interview sheets to the kids — the purpose is to help children feel less awkward in viewing the filmstrip with their parent and to put the parent in touch with the feelings they experienced as they entered puberty. Give them time to complete the interview and then direct them to the filmstrip area.

D. After the filmstrip give the kids time to fill out their four questions on the back of the interview sheet. Give out the parent handout, allow time for reading it and ask for questions and discussions.

INTERVIEW YOUR MOM OR DAD OR BOTH OF THEM

1. When did you start growing up? What changes do you remember happening first?

2. Were you one of the first in your group to develop, or one of the last? How did it feel?

3. What is the most awkward experience you can remember from your puberty years?

4. What is the most rewarding and reassuring experience you had at that time?

5. What did you like most about your body during puberty? What did you like the least?

6. Did you get teased about the body changes that were happening to you?

7. Did you tease other kids about their bodies?

8. Who were your best friends when you were my age? Why did you like them?

9. Did any adults answer your questions about sex at that time? Where did you go for information?

10. When did you finally feel all grown up?

Used by permission. **Growing Up Boys** by Wernette, Hansen and Taylor. Planned Parenthood of Southern Arizona.

These four questions are for you to write an answer to after you see the filmstrip.

1. One thing I think is really great about the way God designed my body is...

2. Something I learned which I didn't know before...

3. What I would still like to know.

4. What worries me about growing up is...

E. In large group, ask some parents and kids to respond aloud to the first two questions on the back of the interview sheets.

F. Remind everyone to bring baby pictures next week if they have not already done so.

G. Join hands for a circle prayer—weave in Thanksgiving using the responses you receive in E above.

FOR PARENTS

Review the filmstrip content in your mind. Jot down anything you didn't want to forget to use as a reinforcement or follow-up in a future discussion with your child.

Sol and Judith Gordon in their book, **Raising a Child Conservatively in a Sexually Permissive World**, emphasize the following:

"There are two areas where parents must accept responsibility: preparing girls for the onset of menstruation, and preparing boys for nocturnal emissions. The child should know well in advance, so that the events do not come as traumatic surprises. And girls should be told about nocturnal emissions, just as boys should be told about menstruation. In fact, girls and boys should be informed fully of these and other developments affecting the opposite sex as well as their own.

When a girl is no older than ten, a mother or female relative should specifically demonstrate the proper method of using sanitary napkins. The demonstration should be accompanied by a very positive explanation of menstruation as a normal and healthy bodily process that all girls first experience between the ages of eleven and fifteen or so. It is vital that the young girl look upon her growth into womanhood as a positive step in her development.

Also around the age of ten, boys should be told by either the mother or the father that wet dreams happen to almost all boys and are a normal stage of male development, usually first experienced between the ages of eleven and fifteen or so. The boy should be told that you understand his bedclothes and linens may get wet, and that he can put them privately into the hamper. It should be made clear that wet dreams are related to sexual impulses and thoughts and will occur less frequently as he gets older. By the time he has opportunities for regular sexual outlets, they are likely to cease altogether."

Did the filmstrip do an adequate job of covering this for your child or will it need more explaining? You may want to weave this into your discussion following their four questions.

Planned Parenthood has several good brochures for children—you will need to read them and decide if and when they would be appropriate for your child. For boys, "Growing Up Boys," and for girls, "The Perils of Puberty," are in a style and format attractive to kids.

SESSION FOUR

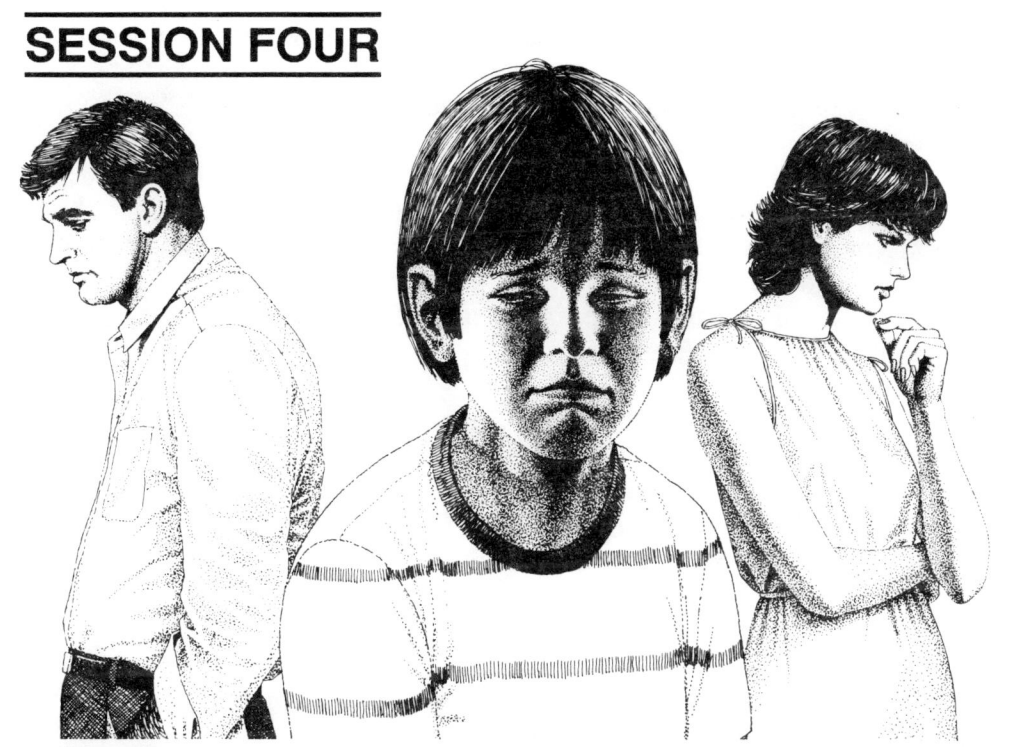

WHEN THE GOOD GIFT OF SEX IS ABUSED

OBJECTIVE: To prepare children who may experience abusive situations in the future and to open doors for those who may need a place to talk about past or ongoing experiences.

To create a forum for discussing how A.I.D.S. spreads.

PREPARATION:
1. Make copies of skits. You will need to get a copy of NO MORE SECRETS FOR ME by Oralee Watcher to be turned into skits to be acted out by parents. Copies can be made of individual chapters for drama purposes but should be collected to avoid copyright violation.

CHOOSE FROM THE FOLLOWING CHAPTERS

    a. "Just in Case" page 15ff — seven separate copies. Highlight parts for Nickie, Mom, Gus, Kevin, Gordy, Judy and Narrator
    b. "What If" page 26ff — four separate copies. Highlight parts for Greg, Marty, Vince, and Narrator

c. "Promise Not to Tell" page 36ff—four separate copies. Highlight parts for Beth, Maureen, and Mrs. De Martino. Narrator should READ parts about Maureen and Pete through "after school the next day..." page 40.

2. Contact a local A.I.D.S. Speaker's bureau through a hospital or community agency. They can provide brochures and a speaker about A.I.D.S. A school nurse, Blood Bank or physician could help. Make it clear that the presentation is to dispel myths about how A.I.D.S. is transmitted and should be very brief.

3. Collect books and videos about Sexual Abuse for display. Use public library and video stores.

4. Make nametags for children's skit and parents skits. Children's nametags should be paired by colors with silly names like "Tony Tinselteeth" or "Nerdy Norton." The starting person can be "Daniel Druggie" and one for a "baby" can be "Innocent Child."

SETUP: As people arrive, collect all the baby pictures, being sure all are marked with names.

NOTE: Up to now no mention has been made about consistent attendance because it has been assumed that families will be committed to the total program. It would be particularly important to note any absences and be sure the children who are not in attendance get a "make-up" session for the five principles taught in this lesson. It should not be presumed that church families are immune to this problem. Arranging a make-up can be stated positively:

"I'm sure you want your son/daughter to be fully aware of their ability to handle this and of our church's concern for their welfare."

CLASSTIME

A. Gather the children together in the horseshoe BEHIND their parents. Read aloud from Psalm 139:13-15 (Jer) emphasizing how wonderfully God made us. Our bodies, even if we have disabilities, are a good creation of God. Let kids stand up behind seated parents and give them a neck rub. Ask the kids to remember back to when they were preschoolers— they may have taken baths with children of the opposite sex or girls might remember running in the sprinklers without swimsuit tops. Remind them that now that they are older they do cover their genitals and that we sometimes refer to a girl's breasts and both boys' and girls' pubic area as "private parts." These are what we cover with a swim suit. We don't cover them because they are sinful or bad, but because they are private — just ours alone.

B. Explain to the group that the parents now need some time to go prepare a skit. Be sure as they divide up that the characters correspond to the people available as much as possible. Be sensitive to putting a strong enough man in group #2 to play "Marty." Alert parents to be aware of their own feelings as they read their parts — anger, shame, embarrassment, etc. Explain materials for name placards. Dismiss parents to three places for a reading and run-through. Assure them that they may come listen in as they finish their practice.

C. Gather the children together in a cluster near the blackboard. While parents are gone, you can explain the five principles of Sexual Abuse Prevention. Children may have had similar lessons at school assemblies, but it is important that they know this is a topic appropriate to discuss in their congregation.

   1. (Review — **Your body is God's good creation**)

   2. Good Feelings — Uh-oh feelings: Ask for several examples of good feelings we get when we are touched (neck rubs, good night kiss or hug, licks from a puppy, a back rub, holding hands walking or praying, etc.) Then ask for experiences they've had when something inside them said, "Uh-oh (breaking a dish, being lost on a hike, spilling paint or milk, or being touched in your private parts)." "Uh-oh" feelings are times when we know something isn't right.

   3. You have a right to say "No." "When you have bad feelings because of something you have done, you usually take some action." Go over the list of things which caused "Uh-oh feelings." Get their ideas about what they would do to remedy the bad feelings. Then ask what they could do if someone touched their private parts or showed them or made them touch an adult's private parts. NO. Emphasize that the first step is to "say no." (Don't use "JUST SAY NO" — it may not be as easy as the word "JUST" implies — and it has been misused in drug programs.) Give examples of relatives, care-givers, paper carrier, etc., as well as strangers in good and bad feelings situations. When should you say "NO" and when is it O.K.? "After you say "NO" you should get out of the situation if this is physically possible. GO means to get away from the person who gives them these bad feelings."

4. Good Secrets—Bad Secrets TELL. Move right into the concept of telling—that touching other people's private parts is serious business and people who try to do that or have done it in the past need help for their problem. The only way they are going to get that help is if children TELL someone who can help. Ask for examples of people who could help (teacher, parent, trusted neighbor, Sunday School teacher, principal, minister, etc.—make a long list for plenty of options). Emphasize that this is not "tattling" and that if the first person doesn't get help and stop the situation, they should tell someone else soon. Summarize points 3 and 4 as NO-GO-TELL.

5. You are not to Blame—the emphasis of this final point is that the victim is not to blame. Even things that happen when we are 9 or 11 years old are not our fault just because we are older and smarter. "Sometimes people we trust or love do things they shouldn't do, but it doesn't make it our fault for loving and trusting them. If they did something to give you an "Uh-oh" feeling, they need help and will get it if you TELL. You will not be blamed for it by counselors or police."

D. By the time you finish these five principles, parents may be drifting back into the room. Allow the children to summarize the four points the parents missed and ask them to be watching for the points during the skits.

E. Have parents act out the skits. After each skit, ask kids to identify NO-GO-TELL. "Did anybody remind the child that he or she was not to blame? Did they lose friends by telling? Who got helped? Would you have resolved it in a different way?" Are there tricks or schemes people use to get children your age to share their bodies? (modeling nude, bribes, group pressure, etc.)

After all three skits have been shared, ask the parents to tell their feelings playing the different parts. How would they feel if their child came and told them something like this had happened?

F. You may want to display adult and children's books and videos available in your church or public library in case families want to share this information with older or younger children. If you know of support groups, church staff or counselors whom parents could turn to for further help, be sure to supply a written handout to everyone. (Many parents are silent victims of childhood abuse and this lesson may bring up very difficult memories.) Make yourself available for further questions and discussions after class.

You will probably need a stretch exercise break here.

G. Introduce your special speaker about A.I.D.S. Distribute age-appropriate brochures and begin to ask questions that get the ball rolling. When questions begin to become sparse, move quickly into the children's skit.

H. Distribute pairs of colored name tags with ridiculous names for boy/girl pairs. Have the pairs stand in front of the group and create a scenario in which one individual gets A.I.D.S. by sharing a dirty drug needle. Through experiences of pre-marital intercourse the virus spreads through the group. Pair off these swinging pairs and choose one to get A.I.D.S. and pair that person up with another victim to keep it spreading. Some couples stick to a monogamous relationship and do not get A.I.D.S. One couple has a baby with A.I.D.S. because of their life choices. At the end ask anyone "infected with A.I.D.S." in the skit to lie down on the floor. Remind the children that A.I.D.S. does not spread through sitting next to someone who has it or other non-bodily fluid contact. A.I.D.S. is not restricted to homosexuals or drug addicts. "When you have sexual intercourse with someone, you are exposing yourself to every sexual partner that person ever had. God intended us to share the good gift of sex with our marriage partner only."

I. If this is an evening course, emphasize that this has been a very serious lesson. Suggest that they make time before bed to have a treat together and discuss something lighter or happier.

Hold hands in a circle and comment on this "good touch." Pray together and be thankful for wonderfully made bodies and people who can help kids in bad situations.

Alternate introduction if class will focus on A.I.D.S. exclusively.

Once upon a time there was a boy with an ability to play the piano that was just incredible. When he started piano lessons as a child, he enjoyed playing from the very first day. Even though he sometimes didn't like practicing, he did so well on his lessons that soon his teacher encouraged him to start giving concerts for his friends. Then he was invited to play for some larger groups and soon his name became known around town. He was well aware that he had this great talent but he didn't get a fat head about it. And he was always careful about where he chose to use the talent. He was invited to play for a fundraising event but he found out the funds wouldn't really be going to a good cause so he said, "no." Another time he was invited to play on a really crummy piano and even though he was offered a lot of money to play, he knew it just wouldn't sound right and he said "no." So people always heard his music in the best places and at the best times and when they heard great piano playing on tapes or records, they thought to themselves, "Someday my friend will be playing those places."

In that same school there was a girl who was a terrific runner. When she used to run races with her friends in the back yard or across the school playground, she always won. She even began to beat kids who were in the upper grades and when she went to Junior High a coach encouraged her to be on the track team. She worked hard at her running skills. She listened to the coach's advice, ate the right foods, got the right amount of sleep and practiced and practiced her starts, her endurance skills and her final kicks. She had the opportunity to run on a track team from a private club but she decided to check it out first. She found out that some of the people who ran the club were prejudiced against letting certain kinds of kids from certain families be on the team and she decided she didn't want to run for a club like that.

She looked for the best places to use her running skills and worked her way up in area races until she became well known in the Junior Olympic circuit. Once she was given the chance to run in a big race but the track was muddy and she thought it might make her slip and fall and injure herself. So she passed it up. It was hard to turn it down because she loved running so much but she decided to wait for a better track. She was glad she did when another better race came along the next weekend and she was in great shape.

Each of these kids was given a great gift...one had the gift for playing beautiful music and the other was a gifted runner. Each of them knew the best way to use their gift, to take care of it and to share it with others. They also knew that there were certain places and times that it was better not to share their special gift and to wait until the right time came along. Their ability to wait until the appropriate time, the time that would be best for them, sometimes took patience and discipline. But in the long run, they were glad they had waited.

Each of you have been given some special skills and talents as well. And you have been given a wonderful gift that God created and said, from the very beginning of creation, "this is very good." Does anyone know what that gift is? Your body. And that gift has many parts that have to work together and have to be taken care of in order to work right.

One part of your body and one part of who you are as a whole person is your sex organs and your sexuality. As you get older you are going to find that there are a lot of people who have some ideas of how you should use this gift from God. Some of those ideas are for their selfish reasons but they are not good for you.

Tonight I had intended to talk mainly about grownups or older teenagers who might try to abuse your body by asking you to do things that make you feel uncomfortable. But most of you have had some training about this in school and so we are just going to do a quick review of this subject we call Sexual Abuse. I am going to see if you remember the steps to get yourself out of a situation or to take care of such a situation if you have been unable to get out of it in the past. Just this past week I met a young man who was abused by a camp counselor when he was just a little older than you so you still need to hear some of these precautions.

Does anyone know one of the ways you are taught to get out of these situations: NO – GO – TELL. (see page 31)

Good feelings/Bad feelings
You have a right to say "no"
Good secrets/Bad secrets
YOU ARE NOT TO BLAME!

Instead of having parents put on skits for you tonight about these ideas, I am going to tackle another subject that you already know a little about. I am not as informed about this as I could be. One thing I hope you have learned in this class is: if you have a question, go ask someone who can give you the correct answer...not your best friend.

Introduce the guest speaker to make a short presentation about how A.I.D.S. is transmitted. Allow time for questions afterwards.

There are also other Sexually Transmitted Diseases being shared by people who share their bodies in sexual relations with more than one person. 45%...that's 45 out of every 100 sexually active teens in this country have a disease called Chlymidia. A lot of them don't even know they have it but it causes girls to be unable to have children (we call this sterility) when they grow up to be women and really want children.

You may wish to have kids perform the skit on page 30 (H).

These aren't things we are just sharing with you to scare you. The best reason to wait until you are married to have sexual relations with another person is not to prevent diseases but because that is part of God's plan for the best way to get to know someone. Boys and girls who take time getting to know each others feelings and hobbies and likes and dislikes, who really listen to each other and enjoy doing sports, and games and dates together, really get to know a lot about each other's whole person. Kids who think they can really get to know a person best by having sexual intercourse with them soon discover they don't really know much about their partner at all and in most cases, they are left with no partner and a lot of bad feelings (if they are lucky). And sometimes girls end up with a baby to take care of and no job or education to pay for caring for that baby. (And sometimes no daddy around.) Some of you may have relatives or friends who have been in that situation.

Every day you and I face choices. When you are your age it may only be deciding what to wear to school, what video tape to play and whether or not to do a good job on your homework or let it slide. These are practice runs for other decisions, even more important decisions you will be making about how to use your athletic abilities, your musical skills, your gift of sexuality, and your brain. All of these are gifts from God. You can let God know how grateful you are by using these gifts wisely or you can disappoint God by dragging these gifts out in the wrong places. You will have to decide these things on your own but you can turn to your parents, counselors, fellowship advisors, grandparents, and even your pastor when you want to talk it over with someone.

It isn't just based on A.I.D.S. or S.T.D.'s or pregnancy that we make decisions. It's basically how we feel about God and God's part in our lives. That's something you'll think about and grow to understand more and more about as you mature. It's exciting and scary but it is also nice to know that even when you make some lousy decisions and mess up sometimes, God will still be waiting to have you come back, tell Him you are sorry, forgive you and let you start all over again.

SESSION FIVE

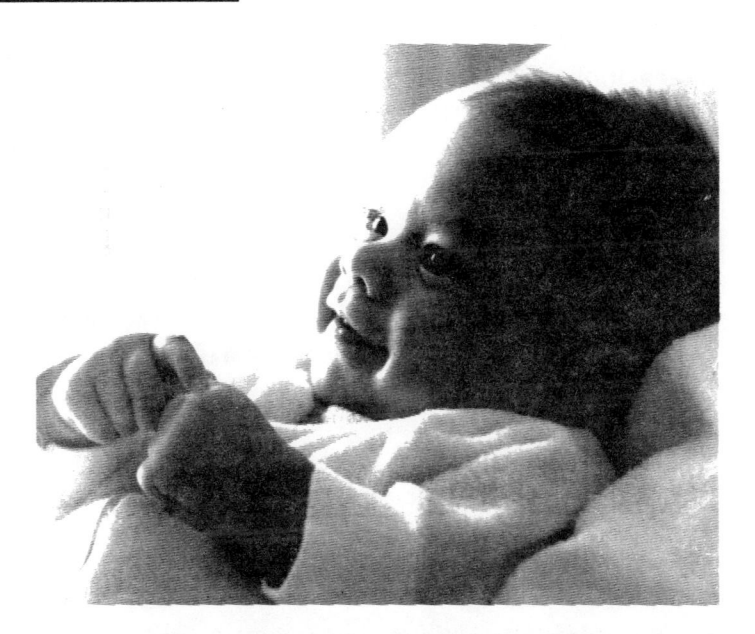

HOW DID I GET HERE?

OBJECTIVE: To gain an understanding of how babies are formed and how happy these parents are to have their particular child in the family.

PREPARATIONS:
1. Rent and preview film: "When Life Begins" CRM—McGraw Hill Films (15 min.)
2. Make copies of parent question sheet.
3. Create displays of baby pictures—use a bulletin board of poster boards with corner mounts so pictures are not damaged. Put a number by each picture (post-it notes work well).
4. Create a numbered answer sheet to correspond to baby picture display. Provide copies and pencils for all.
5. If you wish to have prizes for the picture "contest" fill a small baby bottle with jelly beans or a baby sock with a "Baby Ruth" bar.
6. Make an accurate master list for baby pictures.
7. Copy Session 5 "T.V. Log" handout.

SETUP: This would be a good lesson to use nametags again. Set up room with screen and projector. Run "When Life Begins" past the more technical first minutes and prepare to explain that sequence.

CLASSTIME

A. As people enter they should be given a numbered sheet to write down their guesses about the identity of the posted baby pictures. After everyone has had a fair time to write down their answers, use a master list to share the correct identities. You may reward winners or give everyone a snack size Baby Ruth.

B. Before beginning the film, review the scripture used last week. (Psalm 139:13-15 JERUSALEM) If there are adopted children in your group, you will want to make a distinction between "birth mother" and their parents since adoption. It is very helpful to adopted children if an adopted adult also identifies himself/herself.

Warn children that the pictures of the fetus may be "strange" or "weird." The baby being born may seem "gucky" or "gross." But whether they were a Caesarean birth or a vaginal birth, they were just as "yucky" and now look at their pretty baby pictures!

C. Show the film or video. Ask for their reactions. What was beautiful, surprising, yucky? Have them look at their fingers, flex their muscles, look at their parent's ear shape or nose and comment again on how wonderfully made they are.

D. Hand out the question sheet for parents. Divide into family groups for them to share answers. (Answers do not need to be written.)

E. Gather again in the large group. At the top of the blackboard or newsprint, make two columns:

Girls could/can   Boys could/can

Ask the parents first to give answers to what girls and boys could do when the parents were in elementary school (50's and 60's). After they've listed things, ask the children to add new things and to tell where the parents list should have crossover arrows added to make the entry appear in both columns in the present.

Point out the changes to both parents and children. Remind them that parents are raising boys and girls in "uncharted" territory—that we have to help each other. You may also wish to add that if so much change has taken place in one generation just think how hard it must be to sort out the first century rules in the Bible from the "eternal rules" that are basic to the way we treat each other in relationships.

Session 5 Handout

FOR PARENTS

All of these questions are in regards to the child you have with you today.

Do you remember when you found out you were expecting this child? Or when you heard from the adoption agency? How did you share the news?

What names did you choose for a boy or a girl?

Was there anybody in the family who was hoping for a boy or girl in particular?

Did you know before the birth whether this would be a boy or a girl? (amniocenteses or choice at adoption?)

Were both parents present when the child was born? Tell your child a little about this experience.

When you found out this child was a boy or a girl, how did you feel? Were you more concerned about health, rest, calling relatives at that time?

Can you remember some of the first "gender related" toys your child received?

As your child grew into toddlerhood, did you attribute certain characteristics to being "all girl" or " all boy" or were you trying to downplay those stereotypes? Tell your child about this.

As your child entered preschool and elementary school, what changes did you see in their "masculinity" or "femininity?"

What changes do you notice happening now? Tell your child how glad you are they are a boy or a girl and why you are glad.

Session 5 Sample Homework Handout

T.V. log for week of _____

Show or commercial	Males	Females
Examples:		
Cosby Show	a. dad-doctor b. son-student, basketball player	a. mom-lawyer b. daughter-student, roller skater c. daughter-college student d. daughter-Jr. High student
hot dogs	a. boy and dad cook & eat hotdogs	
6 p.m. news	a. sportscaster b. newscaster	a. weather reporter b. newscaster
Coca-Cola	a. grandfather reminisces b. grandson-plays soccer	
Family Ties	a. father-PBS wkr. b. son-business student c. son-preschooler	a. mother-architect b. daughter-college student in fashion design c. daughter-H.S. student/athlete

Session 5 Homework Handout

T.V. log for week of_____

Show or commercial **Males** **Females**

F. For homework, ask participants to take home a T.V. viewing sheet and keep it by the T.V. to record all the roles they see men/boys and women/girls play this week. "Record as many shows or commercials as you see but don't add extra T.V. to your life. Parents may not correct kids' spelling on the chart and must be honest about how much T.V. they watch. Take as many sheets as you think you'll need." Show an example from the back of this section.

G. Close in a prayer being thankful for life, our wonderful bodies and being boys/girls and men/women.

H. Remind people to retrieve baby pictures and T.V. logs, and to return name tags.

SESSION SIX

BEING ALIKE, BEING LIKED, BEING MYSELF

OBJECTIVE: To discover the qualities we admire in boys and girls, men and women; to compare those qualities with T.V. and school norms; to discuss peer pressure and its qualities, and to list adults we can talk to when we need encouragement. To celebrate being able to learn from each other and to encourage feedback.

PREPARATION:
1. Gather Bibles and butcher paper, markers, and pencils.
2. Provide cookies, punch, cups, and napkins.
3. Find collages from Session 1.
4. Copy class evaluations.

SETUP: Post the three collages from Session 1.

CLASSTIME

A. If you have wallspace, put up two more large butcher papers labeled "T.V.—females" and "T.V.—males." As people enter, provide felt markers for them to list the roles they saw played on T.V. If you don't have wallspace, you may have boys line up on one side to read all the male roles and girls line up on the other side to read the female roles (you'll need to cut the T.V. logs in half for this).

Discuss whether there were any noticeable differences. Invite parents to recall the roles played by men and women in the 50's and 60's and how they've changed. Is it better, worse or too radically different to judge?

B. Divide the class into two groups—boys with their parents and girls with their parents. Provide Bibles, newsprint and markers and ask each group to create a list of admirable qualities for boys and girls. On the newsprint list the scriptures for starters, but encourage them to add their scripture ideas also.

Girls: I Corinthians 13:4-7; Proverbs Chapter 31; Galatians 5:22-26; Ephesians 4:29,31-32; I Peter 3:3-4.

Boys: I Corinthians 13:4-7; I Timothy 3:1-7; Galatians 5:22-26; Ephesians 4:29, 31-32.

C. In the large group, share the lists and ask people to give examples of the forces that work against developing these qualities. This may be difficult to get rolling, but give some examples and encourage parents to admit what keeps them from "measuring up" to God's yardstick.

D.

1) Try to summarize by creating a verbal picture of a person who would make God's spirit happy (as opposed to Ephesians 4:30) How would this person dress? What would they spend their money on? How would they choose their friends? Who would they consult in making decisions? Would this person be popular at your school?

"How do you balance being "with-it" so you feel good about yourself and still measuring up to God's yardstick? Do you have to be "out of it" to follow scripture?"

2) Use similar questions to **summarize a popular T.V. person** and a popular person at school. **Is a popular person at school more like God's yardstick or a T.V. yardstick?**

E. Spend some time discussing "peers" and "peer pressure." Why is it natural to want to be liked? "It is **natural to be** influenced by the people we admire so it is important to make **good choices about who** we'll spend our time with, who we'll look up to, etc. **When parents say "no" to a particular** record or movie or group of kids, it is **because they've looked at God's** yardstick and found these people don't "measure up." **Sometimes parents** are pretty quick to judge by someone's dress and language and you'll need to talk about a person's other qualities and whether you could **invite** them to be part of your family setting." Allow kids and parents some time to talk about experiences when peers influenced them to be a better person or to do something that would "make God sad."

F. "Sometimes parents aren't available to talk to or you need a 'second opinion.'" Make a list of alternative people kids could trust to share their feelings or ask questions. Would parents expect this other party to share their conversation or would they let the other person keep it confidential? Encourage kids to keep talking to their parents as they have in this class.

G. Hand out the evaluation sheets. As they begin to fill them out, set out cookies and punch for a closing celebration. As people finish their evaluations, they can come get refreshments and leave the evaluations in a box.

H. Ask everyone to put down their cookies and punch to put their arms around each other's shoulders in a circle closing. Ask for "popcorn prayer"—anyone may share a short prayer of thanksgiving or concern. Close with thanksgiving for the entire class experience.

Sometimes kids want to take home the collage. Have some large scissors available to divide some for multiple requests.

Class Evaluation (sample)

I am: a child   a parent

I am: male   female

Here are the six topics we covered. Circle the title of the ones you attended. Then rate it on a scale of 1 to 5.

1. Don't repeat this one.
2. Include it but improve it.
3. It was O.K.
4. This was a good lesson.
5. Keep it just as it was—great!

1. Everyone has something to say about sex
We looked at magazines and made collages. We filled out questionnaires about the things we talk about with friends and what's good and bad about our age.

RATING: 1 2 3 4 5
Comments:

2. Does everyone feel as different as I do?
This lesson was about the changes we begin to experience in our feelings—our need for privacy, close friends, and our maleness or femaleness. We did a stand up-sit down game about things we like and how we look. We saw a filmstrip with kids experiencing change and we thought about being kids again or about becoming 18.

RATING: 1 2 3 4 5
Comments:

3. Good grief! What's happening to me?
This lesson was about physical changes. We recalled the growth of the children from age two to the present. Kids interviewed their parents about the parent's physical changes. We saw the filmstrip "How You Got to be You" or "The New You." The parents received booklets for their future use.

RATING: 1 2 3 4 5
Comments:

4. Childhood Sexual Abuse Prevention/A.I.D.S.
We started with neck rubs. Then the parents went off to practice three skits from No More Secrets For Me. The kids learned five basic lessons about prevention and then looked for these in the skits. In a general discussion we brought up tricks strangers may use to lure kids away. We discussed A.I.D.S. and how it is spread through sexual intercourse.

RATING: 1 2 3 4 5
Comments:

5. How Did I Get Here?
We did a guessing game with baby pictures. We saw a film "When Life Begins" about a baby's prenatal development and birth. Parents told kids about their birth and about their maleness/femaleness as an issue. On newsprint we gathered ideas about the changing ideas of what boys and girls can do and be.

RATING: 1 2 3 4 5
Comments:

6. Being Alike, Being Liked, Being Myself
We compared the TV image of men and women with the qualities God looks for in people. We tried to define what popularity is. We discussed who we could go to with questions in the future.

RATING: 1 2 3 4 5
Comments:

In the future, I think this class should be taught to:

    4th grade boys, 5th grade boys, 6th grade boys
    and/or 4th grade girls, 5th grade girls, 6th grade girls

Which portion was most helpful?

Which portion was least helpful?

Were there concerns we didn't address satisfactorily?

Any additional suggestions or comments?

BIBLIOGRAPHY

BOOKS FOR CHILDREN

THE FACTS OF LIFE, Jonathan Miller and David Pelham. (Viking Penguin Inc. New York, NY, 1984) Three dimensional illustrations depict all the wonders of human reproduction.

HOW YOU GOT TO BE YOU, Carol Greene. (Concordia, St. Louis, 1982) Book three of a six part series for all ages and parents. Corresponds to Filmstrip of same name.

NO MORE SECRETS FOR ME, Oralee Watcher. (Little, Brown and Co., Boston, 1983) An introduction and four stories about children in situations of sexual abuse.

PREPARING FOR ADOLESCENCE, Dr. James Dobson. (Vision House, Ventura, CA, 1978) Includes chapters on self-esteem, bodily changes, emotions, love, etc.

THE WONDERFUL WAY THAT BABIES ARE MADE, Larry Christenson. (Bethany House Publishers, Minneapolis, MN, 1982) Illustrated with large print for younger children, smaller print paragraphs for 9-14 year olds and a special section on adoption.

BOOKS FOR PARENTS AND TEACHERS

THE GIFT OF SEX, Clifford and Joyce Penner. (Word Inc., Waco, TX, 1981) A handbook that celebrates the spiritual, emotional, and physical aspects of Christian sexuality in marriage.

RAISING A CHILD CONSERVATIVELY IN A SEXUALLY PERMISSIVE WORLD, Sol and Judith Gordon. (Simon and Schuster, New York, 1983) A "secular" book which dispels the mysteries surrounding adolescent sexuality and promotes healthy and responsible attitudes about sexuality.

YOUTHWORKER, Winter 1985, Volume I, Number IV. (Youth Specialties, El Cajon, CA) This edition of this quarterly journal features eight articles on sexuality from the church worker's point of view.

PAMPHLETS FOR STUDENTS

THE PERILS OF PUBERTY. (RMPP Publications, 1525 Josephine St., Denver, Colorado, 80206) A very candid pamphlet for girls. Some parents may find it too frank. Available from a local Planned Parenthood Office.

GROWING UP BOYS, Wernette, Hansen and Taylor. (Planned Parenthood of Southern Arizona, Inc. 127 S. Fifth Ave., Tucson, AZ, 85701) A very candid pamphlet for boys. Some parents may find it too frank. Available from a local Planned Parenthood Office in English or Spanish.

GROWING UP GIRLS, Wernette, Hansen, Taylor and Bowen. (Planned Parenthood of Southern Arizona, Inc. 127 S. Fifth Ave., Tucson, AZ, 85701) A very candid pamphlet for girls. Some parents may find it too frank. Available from a local Planned Parenthood Office. Bilingual text.

CHANGING, booklets for boys and girls, published by Proctor and Gamble and available through the public schools.

HELPFUL INFORMATION ON A.I.D.S.

To call for information dial: 1-800-342-AIDS

From a packet "A.I.D.S. Prevention Guide" for Parents and Other Adults Concerned About Youth--there are two good sheets of guidelines worth writing for. One is entitled "Deciding What To Say To Younger Children (Late Elementary and Middle School Aged)" and the other is called "Information For Young People (Late Elementary and Middle School Aged)." From Dept. 7 Health & Human Services, Public Health Services, Centers for Disease Control, P.O. Box 6003, Rockville, MD 20850.

From the publication **MMWR** (Morbidity and Mortality Weekly Report), the article entitled "Guidelines for Effective School Health Education To Prevent the Spread of A.I.D.S." Supplement Jan. 29, 1988, Vol. 37, No. S-2. From the U.S. Department of Health and Human Services, Public Health Service, Centers for Disease Control, Center for Health Promotion and Education, Atlanta, GA 30333.